Keyboard 2

INTRODUCTION

Why did you buy this book, too?

You bought it because you love learning to play the keyboard. And we're glad—it's a great instrument!

We assume that you've already completed (and reviewed a couple hundred times) **FastTrack™ Keyboard 1**. If not, please consider going through it first. (We'd hate to cover something before you're ready.)

In any case, this book picks up right where **Book 1** ended. You'll learn lots more chords, plenty of cool techniques, and an in-depth look at the most popular styles in today's music. And, of course, the last section of all the **FastTrack™** books is the same so that you and your friends can form a band and jam together!

So, if you still feel ready for this book, finish your pizza, put the cat outside, take the phone off the hook, and let's jam...

Always remember the three Ps: **patience, practice** and **pace yourself**. We'll add one more to this list: be **proud of yourself** for a job well-done.

ABOUT THE AUDIO

We're glad you noticed the added bonus—audio tracks! Each music example in the book is included, so you can hear how it sounds and play along when you're ready. Take a listen whenever you see this symbol: ❶

Each audio example is preceded by one measure of "clicks" to indicate the tempo and meter. Pan right to hear the keyboard part emphasized. Pan left to hear the accompaniment emphasized. As you become more confident, try playing along with the rest of the band.

To access audio visit:
www.halleonard.com/mylibrary
Enter Code
1329-6414-2675-1414

ISBN 978-0-7935-7545-9

7777 W. BLUEMOUND RD. P.O. BOX 13819 MILWAUKEE, WI 53213

Visit Hal Leonard online at
www.halleonard.com

LESSON 1
You wanna rock!

How you play is as important (if not more important) as **what** you play. In this book, we'll show you some common styles used in today's music. You can apply these styles to almost any song.

As we introduce each style, notice how the following musical elements change:

 Chord progression

 Rhythmic groove

 Note choice

We'll also learn new chords, rhythms, and techniques as we go. Let's get started with an all-time favorite...

Rock 'n' Roll

Rock music comes in many styles—classic rock, blues rock, easy rock, hard rock, heavy metal. Its roots date from the 1950s with such legends as Elvis Presley, Jerry Lee Lewis, and The Beatles. Track 1 is an example of '50s rock 'n' roll. Listen and then play along:

◆ 1 Golden Oldie

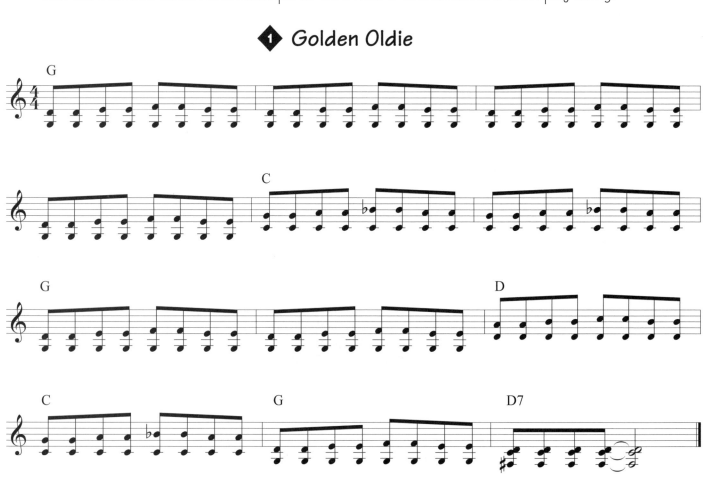

It's Here to Stay

Hard Rock and Heavy Metal

Moving up through the decades, rock music transformed into a harder sound found in the music of Led Zeppelin, Aerosmith, and Van Halen. The following examples imitate hard rock and heavy metal styles:

All Along the Sidewalk

Go Ahead!

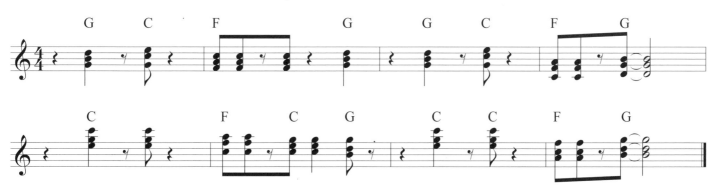

Glam Rock

Rock music isn't (usually) slow. Sometimes you'll want to play faster than eighth notes but in the same tempo. How's that done? Welcome to the world of sixteenths...

Sixteenth Notes

These have two flags or beams: ♪ ♪ ♪ ♪ = 𝅘𝅥𝅯𝅘𝅥𝅯𝅘𝅥𝅯𝅘𝅥𝅯

Sixteenth rests look like eighth rests but with (you're way ahead of us!) two flags: 𝄿

Yuck, more math...

Two sixteenths equal one eighth (just like fractions), and four sixteenths equal one quarter. Here's a diagram showing the relationship of all the rhythmic values you've learned:

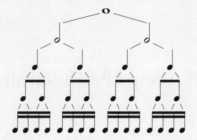

To count sixteenths, divide the beat even further by counting "1 e & a, 2 e & a, 3 e & a, 4 e & a":

| 1(&) | 2(&) | 3 | & | 4 | & | 1 e & a | 2 e & a | 3 e & a | 4 e & a |

Listen to track 6 (with steady quarter note clicks throughout) to hear this new faster rhythm.

◆ **6 Progressively Faster**

1(&)   2(&)   3   &   4   &   1 e & a 2 e & a 3   &   4 (&)   etc.

Now try playing it. Remember to play slowly at first and speed up the tempo only as it becomes easier.

You gotta know how to play chords with sixteenths, too...

7 Rockin' Sixteenths

And, of course, let's try a song with sixteenths in the melody...

☞ METER ALERT: The next tune is in 2/4 meter. (Don't panic—it's nothing really new!) A quarter note still equals one beat and each measure simply contains two beats.

8 Arkansas Traveler

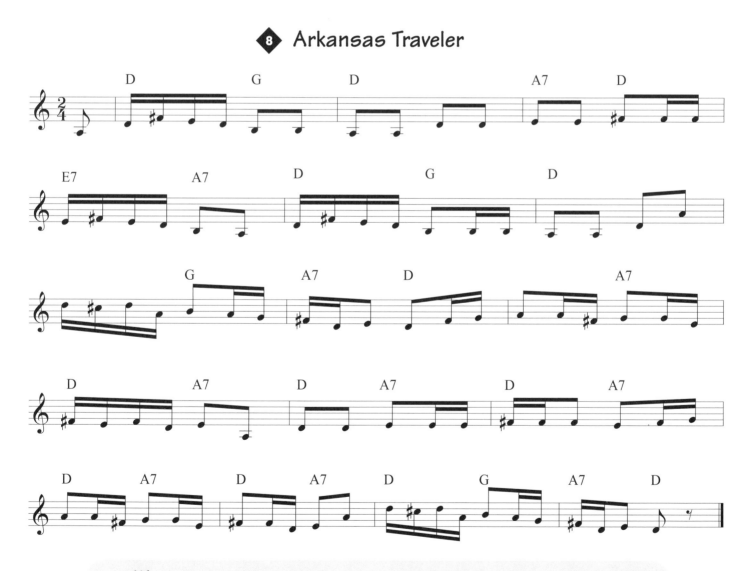

We like to encourage breaks on a regular basis, and this is no exception.
Take five and we'll see you back here for Lesson 2.

LESSON 2

Keys, please...

Remember **key signatures** from Book 1? These tell you two important things about a song:

1 Notes to play sharp or flat throughout the piece

2 Song's key

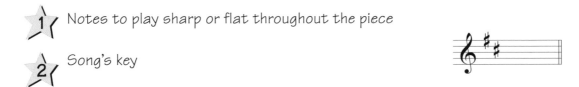

A song's **key** is determined by the scale used to create the song. For example, a song based on the G major scale is said to be in the **key of G**. And since the G major scale contains one sharp (F♯), the key signature will show one sharp on the F-line.

Here are some common (and easy) keys:

Key of C

...based on the C major scale, which has no sharps or flats:

◆ 9 I've Been Rockin' on the Railroad

NOTE: The key of C looks like there is no key signature, since there are no sharps or flats.

Key of G

...based on the G major scale, which has one sharp—F#:

◆10 Shenandoah

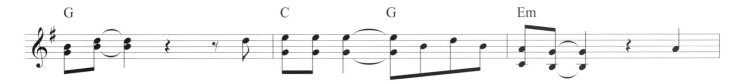

Key of F

...based on the F major scale, which has one flat—B♭:

◆11 Oh, Susanna

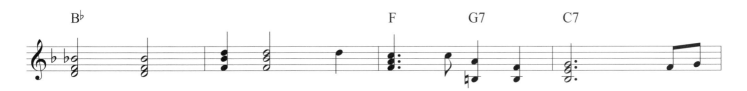

This one has two sharps (F# and C#) and is based on (you guessed it!) the D major scale:

12 The Yellow Rose of Texas

Key of Bb

This one has two flats and is based on the Bb major scale:

13 America, The Beautiful

PRIMARILY SPEAKING

Each key has a set of **primary chords**, the chords most commonly used for songs in that key. (Of course, other chords will also be played, but these are the primary ones.)

A key's primary chords are usually the **root** ("tonic"), **fourth** ("subdominant"), and **fifth** ("dominant"). Roman numerals are often used to name these chords. Find them by counting up the scale from the root of the key:

Key	Chord / Scale Tone							
	I			IV	V		*	
Key of C	C	Dm	Em	F	G	Am	Bdim	C
Key of F	F	Gm	Am	B♭	C	Dm	Edim	F
Key of G	G	Am	Bm	C	D	Em	F♯dim	G
Key of D	D	Em	F♯m	G	A	Bm	C♯dim	D
Key of B♭	B♭	Cm	Dm	E♭	F	Gm	Adim	B♭

* chord symbol explained later

NOTE: Sometimes the primary V chord is substituted with a seventh chord (V7).

Track 14 employs the primary chords of the key of C…

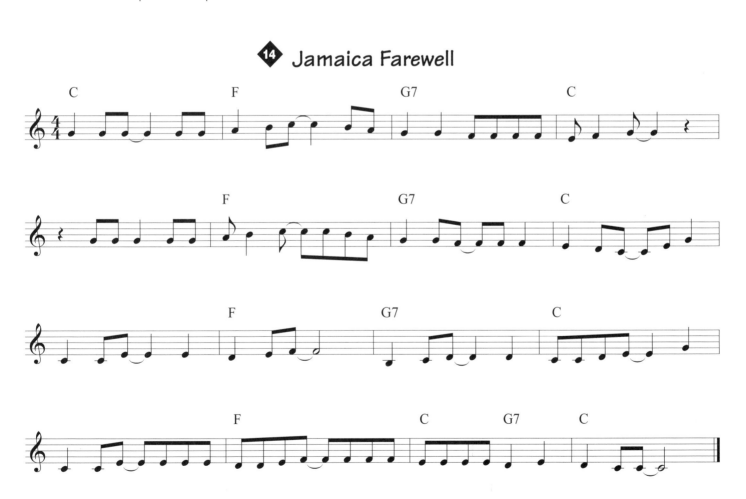

14 Jamaica Farewell

LESSON 3
You've got the blues...

If you haven't heard of the **blues**, then where have you been? It's been around for ages and has been used by such music legends as B.B. King, Eric Clapton, and Muddy Waters. Blues is fun (and easy) to play.

12-Bar Form

The most typical blues uses a form called **12-bar form**. This doesn't mean that the song is only twelve bars (measures) long. Rather, the song uses several 12-bar phrases (or sections) repeated over and over.

Generally, blues songs use the primary chords (I, IV, V) of the key. Listen to the following example of 12-bar blues in "G" on track 15. Then play along...

🔷 15 Blues in "G"

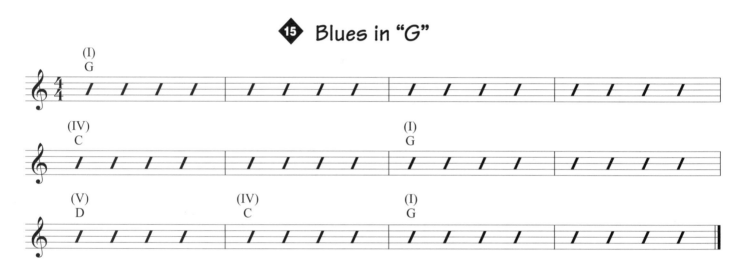

IMPORTANT: Notice the number of measures each chord is played during the 12-bar form. This is the most common 12-bar blues chord progression...

Chord		Measures
I	=	four
IV	=	two
I	=	two
V	=	one
IV	=	one
I	=	two

Turnaround, sit up, and play...

The last two bars of the 12-bar blues progression are sometimes called the **turnaround,** since it "turns" the form back "around" to the beginning. Musicians often vary the turnaround, using different chords or even a written-out riff.

In a minor blues progression (like track 16), the most common turnaround variation uses a major V7 chord in the last measure:

16 Minor Blues

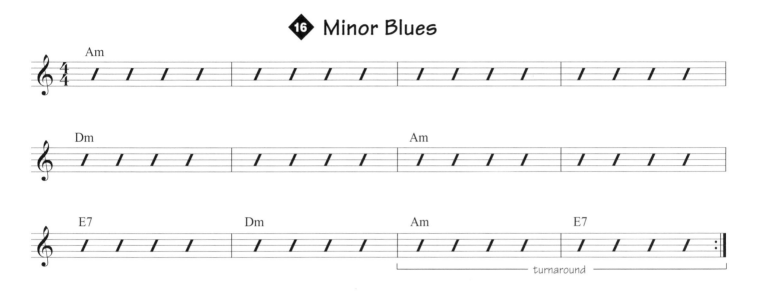

Another variation is to play the IV chord in measure 2. This is called the **quick change,** since you "change" to the IV and "quickly" return to the I.

17 Quick Change Artist

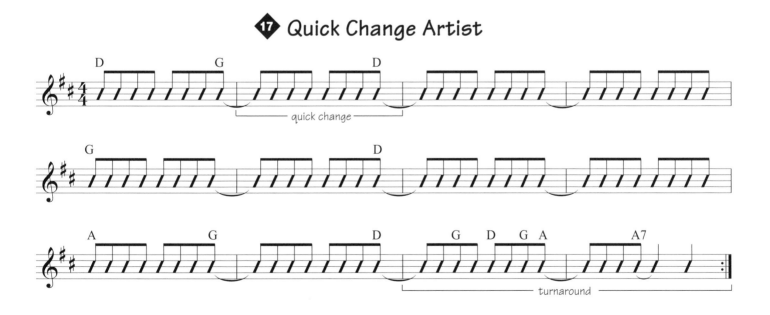

Change is good...

Instead of just slamming the same chord for each measure, try a variation—keep the same root note and simply raise the top two notes up and back on each beat. Try it with track 18...

🔷18 Alternate Blues

Take it a step further...

Now try the same approach, but break the chord—that is, alternate the top two notes with the root on each eighth note:

🔷19 Not So Blue

Time for a solo...

Remember the blues scale from Book 1? Use it to improvise solos over a blues progression. Here's a reminder of that scale and a sample riff based on it:

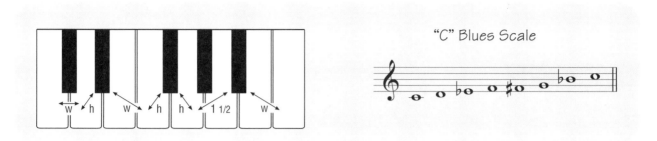

"C" Blues Scale

20 Bluesy Solo

When playing the blues, almost any note sounds good.
So, don't get upset if you play a wrong note occasionally—just say you meant to play that!

LESSON 4
Shut up and shuffle!

The **shuffle feel** is a very common element of rock and blues music. It uses a new rhythmic value called a **triplet**.

Triplets

By now you know that two eighth notes equal one quarter, and four eighth notes equal one half. Guess what? Three eighth notes played in the duration of one beat (or one quarter note) is an **eighth-note triplet**.

An eighth-note triplet is beamed together with a number 3: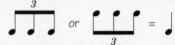

To count a triplet, simply say the word "tri-pl-et" during one beat. Tap your foot to the beat and count out loud as you listen to track 21:

21 Tri-pl-et

count: 1   2   tri - pl - let   4   tri - pl - let   tri - pl - let   3   4   1   2   &   tri - pl - let   4

Here's a perfect example of triplets used in a well-known classical piece. Keep tapping your foot as you listen to and follow the song:

22 Jesu, Joy of Man's Desiring

Now play it yourself. Keep thinking "tri-pl-et, tri-pl-et, tri-pl-et, tri-pl-et" as you tap your foot to the beat...

 You can also use the word "cho-co-late" to help you count triplets. (Of course, this could make you really hungry after counting a long song?!)

Sure—classical can be considered a type of musical style, but we want to keep rockin'. So, moving up a few centuries in music, let's play some triplets in a rock-style shuffle à la Jerry Lee Lewis...

23 Three of a Kind

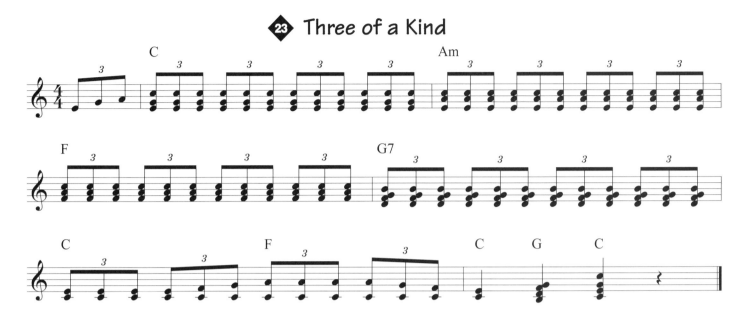

Triplets can also include rests. Most common is to have a rest within the triplet (between two eighth notes):

Once you get the hang of this "bouncy" feel, you'll never forget it...

25 Strawberry

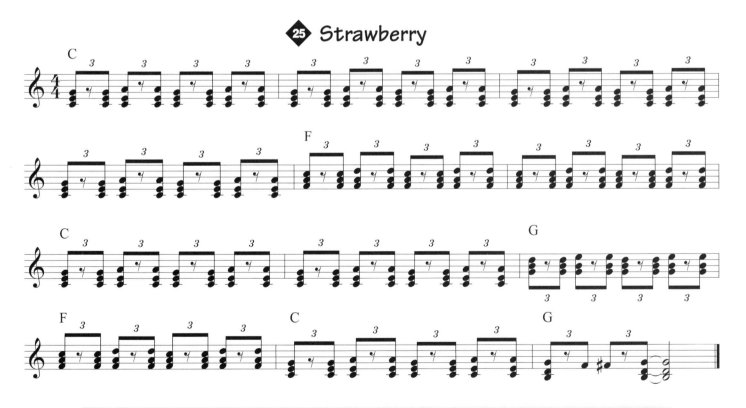

☞ PLAYING TIP: It's an easy variation—just raise your pinkie up and back down. This is a very popular shuffle accompaniment pattern used by early rock 'n' rollers.

3/4...4/4...12/8?

Until this page, you've been playing with time signatures in which the quarter note equaled one beat. Time for something new (change is good!):

12 beats per measure
eighth note (1/8) = one beat

All notes and rests are relative to the value of an eighth note in 12/8 meter:

eighth = one beat   quarter = two beats   dotted quarter = three beats   dotted half = six beats

In 12/8 meter, an eighth note equals one beat and there are twelve beats per measure. But the rhythmic pulse feels like there are four beats per measure. Listen and count along to track 26, and you'll see what we mean:

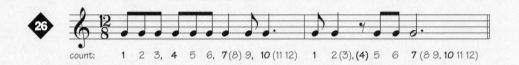

count: 1 2 3, 4 5 6, 7 (8) 9, 10 (11 12)   1   2 (3), (4) 5   6   7 (8 9, 10 11 12)

You'll find 12/8 meter in well-known tunes...

🔷27 Mexican Hat Dance

in ballads...

28 Ballad in 12/8

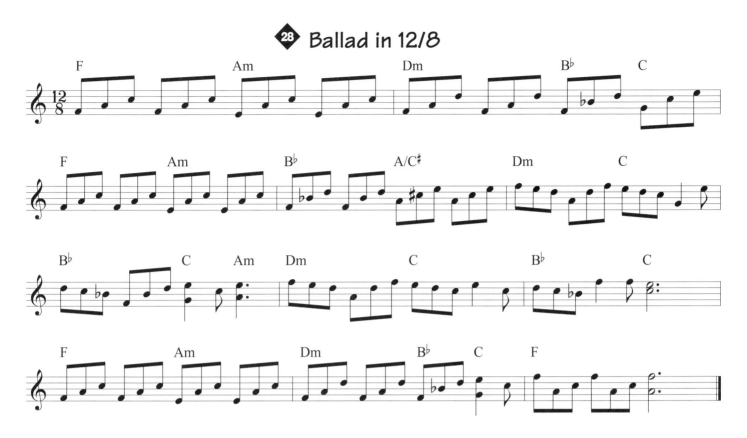

and especially in blues shuffles...

29 Shuffling in Chicago

LISTEN AND COMPARE: The rhythmic feel of track 29 is similar to that of track 25 (on page 15). That's because 12/8 meter is divided into groups of three eighth notes, just like triplets in 4/4 meter.

LET'S GET FANCY!

Want to add some style to your styles? Now's a great time to learn some extended techniques that you've heard (or even experimented playing) but didn't know exactly how to do them.

Grace Note

...looks like this

The little eighth note with a slash through it is the **grace note**. You don't have to count it, because (theoretically) it has no rhythmic value. Instead, you play it very quickly just before the melody note it precedes. Check out track 30 for a better understanding:

30 St. Louis Blues

Grace notes can also precede chords and intervals. They can make a blues jam sound first-class:

31 Graceful Shuffle

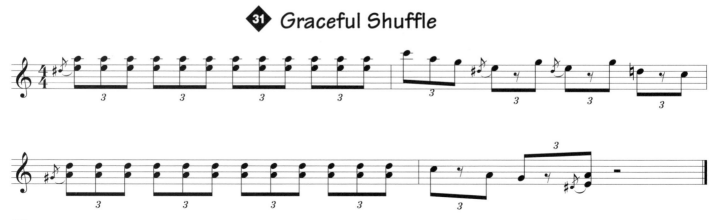

You can also play multiple grace notes. These are beamed together like sixteenths (but again, they have no rhythmic value). As with the single grace note, play them as quickly as possible, as if you are "rolling" into the melody note.

☞ IMPORTANT: Multiple grace notes can be tricky if you don't use correct fingering. We've given you some sample fingering on these two examples.

32 Rags to Riches

Tremolo

...looks like this

You simply alternate between the two interval notes as quickly as possible. Very popular in rock music is the **octave tremolo.** Put your hand in position to play the octave, then quickly rock your hand back and forth.

IMPORTANT: Notes that are tremoloed are shown with the same rhythmic value. However, you only count the value of one of them. That is, a whole-note tremolo will show two whole notes in a measure, but you play the value of one whole note.

33 Fast and Furious

Add a tremolo to a chord—alternate the top two notes with the bottom note (again, as quickly as possible):

34 Chord Tremors

LESSON 5

Pop goes the music!

As we said in the previous lesson, 12/8 meter is great for ballads. And ballads are perhaps most closely related to the next style of music…

Pop

Pop music (short for "popular") covers a wide spectrum. Sometimes called "Adult Contemporary," this style is used by artists like Whitney Houston, Sting, Elton John, and Mariah Carey. This style is typically very melodic and used in lots of ballads:

◆35 Top 40 Ballad

Add a sixth interval below each melody note for an even more melodic and fuller sound. It's easy—simply locate a sixth below the first melody note and "freeze" your hand in this shape to play the rest:

Try it…

◆36 Oh, So Sweet

Of course, not all pop songs are ballads:

37 It Used to be Mine

Slash Chords

A new chord you'll see quite often in pop music is a **slash chord**. These chords indicate a specific bass note to be played. For example, C/G means to play a C chord over a G bass note. When you see a slash in a chord symbol, play the note to the right of the slash with your left hand.

38 Love Song

For the next one, keep your left hand playing eighth notes on the bass note A while the right hand plays the specified chord:

39 Slash 'n' Pop

THEORY OF RELATIVITY

Each major key has a **relative minor key.** The relative minor key is always one and a half steps (a minor third interval) below the major key's root. Why is it relative? Because it has the same key signature as the major key.

One and a half steps below G is E, so E minor is the relative minor to G:

Minor keys also have primary chords, based on the minor scale tones I, IV and V:

	I	*		IV	V			
Key of A minor	Am	Bdim	C	Dm	E7	F	G	Am
Key of D minor	Dm	Edim	F	Gm	A7	Bb	C	Dm
Key of E minor	Em	F#dim	G	Am	B7	C	D	Em

*chord symbol explained later

IMPORTANT: Minor keys use the V7 (major) chord instead of a minor V.

Track 40 looks like it's in the key of G—one sharp. However, since the song has an overall minor sound, it's considered to be in the relative E minor key:

40 House of the Rising Sun

22

When playing a chord progression in the key of G, it's very easy to "shift" to the relative minor key (E minor) and use the minor primary chords over the same melody. Let's try it with the same tune as track 30 (page 18):

41 St. Louis Blues (Minor)

As you can hear, substituting different chords over the same melody can dramatically change the overall sound. This kind of variation is called (think fast!) **chord substitution**. Substituting a major chord with a relative minor is a simple (but effective) form of chord substitution.

Again and again...

Another rockin' chord accompaniment is simply repeating the same chord at a fast rhythm while the band jams. Get your hands ready and start slamming:

42 Over and Over

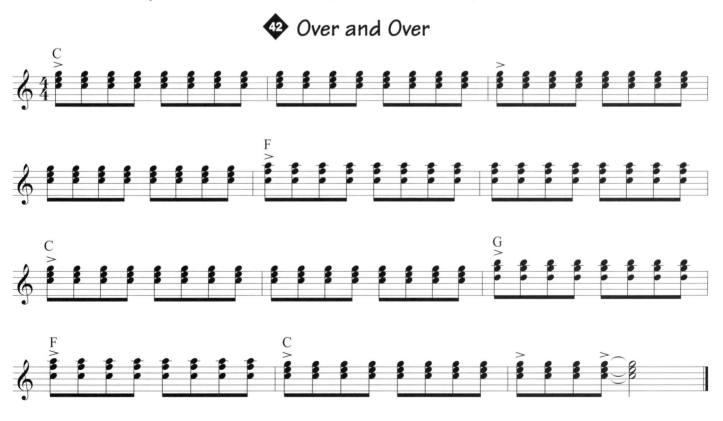

Take a break—call a friend and have them learn another **FastTrack**™ instrument.
But don't dial too fast...you're supposed to rest those fingers!

RHYTHM BREAK

Before we tackle a new style, here's an introduction to a new rhythm...

Dotted Eighth Note

Just like the dotted quarter and dotted half, a **dot** on an eighth note extends the note's value by one half. So, a **dotted eighth note** equals the length of one and a half eighth notes (or one eighth plus one sixteenth).

Dotted eighths are usually connected to a sixteenth, like this:

It's much easier to hear this rhythm than to count it, so listen to track 43 a couple of times:

Then try playing it in a tune:

44 The Darktown Strutters' Ball

The next lesson will incorporate lots of dotted eighth rhythms, since they're great for dancing!

24

LESSON 6
Get on the dance floor!

Like the jitterbug, waltz, and tango of earlier decades, today's music incorporates many styles that really get those feet moving...

R&B

R&B is the short way of saying "rhythm & blues." It's also sometimes called "soul." You'll find this style in the music of Stevie Wonder, Marvin Gaye, The Temptations, and many others.

Play through a couple of riffs with an R&B flair. (It's important to listen to what the rest of the band is doing, too. The drum beat, syncopation, bass line, all contribute to the style being played.)

45 Motown Groove

46 Movin'

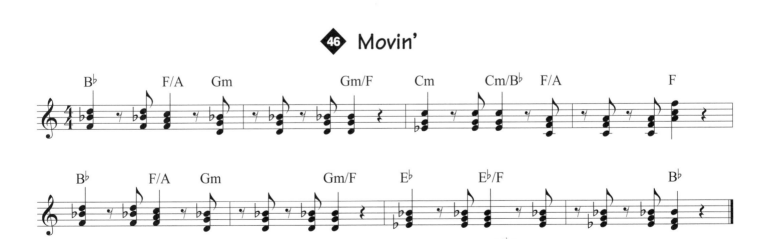

Funk

Funk style can be found in anything from R&B to pop to alternative. You've heard of James Brown, Prince, Rick James, and The Red Hot Chili Peppers, right? They've all used funk style. Listen to both of these tracks several times until you get that "funky feeling"...

CAUTION: Watch out for those dotted eighth-sixteenth patterns. Funk style is full of this kind of rhythm.

47 Funky Keys

48 Funkadelic

26

Here are some more dance styles to help you "get in the groove"...

Disco

Say what you want, but disco just won't die! It came and went in the '70s but resurfaced in the '90s as a major influence on today's dance music. This undeniably unique style incorporates fast rhythms and swirling keyboard sounds. Track 49 is merely an example:

49 Disco Daze

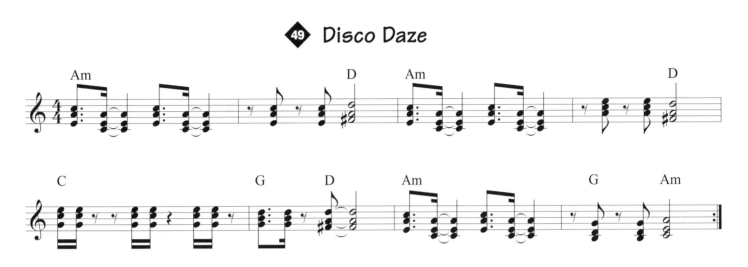

Hip-Hop

A descendant of rap music, the hip-hop style is heavily influenced by reggae, R&B, funk, and (sometimes) rock. Such artists as Snoop Doggy Dogg, TLC, Warren G, and many others have made hip-hop a mainstream musical style.

50 Non-stop Hip Hop

COOL SOUNDS: If you have an electric keyboard, try track 50 again with a "fuzzy synth" sound. Cool, huh?

MORE ON RHYTHM

Instead of three eighth notes, a triplet will sometimes contain one quarter and one eighth played in the duration of one beat. In place of the eighth note beam, a bracket is used:

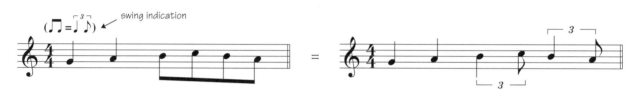

Notice that this sounds like the shuffle feel. This rhythm is also the basis for another type of musical style...

Swing

Not only a dance craze from the '30s, **swing** is a specific kind of rhythm. You can swing any melody or rhythm simply by playing eighth notes as if they were a quarter-eighth triplet:

Listen to the following examples (track 52 is "straight"; track 53 is with a swing beat):

52 53 Swing This!

You try it. Remember, the first eighth of each beat should sound slightly longer than the second. (Bet you can't play it without dancing!)

LESSON 7

In perfect harmony!

You already know lots of great chords, including some major, minor and seventh chords. Let's briefly take a look at how chords are formed (so we can make some more)…

Building Chords

Generally, major and minor chords contain three notes—**root, third**, and **fifth**. The difference between the two chord types is simply one half step. That is, the **third** of a **major** chord is lowered one half step to make a **minor** chord. Take a look…

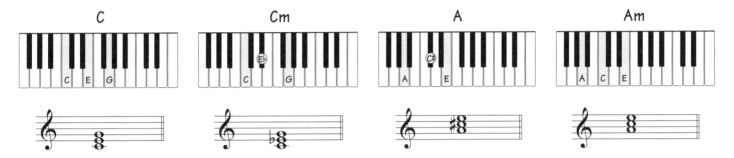

Make any major chord minor simply by lowering the third by one half step; make any minor chord major by raising the third by one half step.

☞ IMPORTANT: Almost all chord types are related in this kind of way. That is, you simply raise, lower, add, or subtract intervals to a major or minor chord to make a new type of chord.

Remember how to make a seventh chord? Simply add the note that is one whole step lower than the root of a major or minor chord:

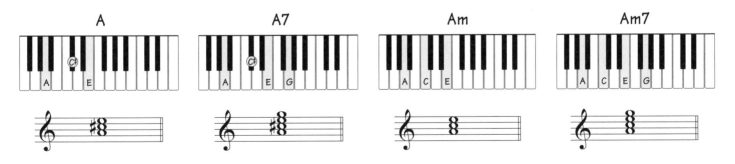

Wanna learn to make some new chords? Turn the page…

Augmented

Any major chord can be made into an **augmented** chord simply by raising the fifth by a half step. The suffix for an augmented chord is "aug" or "+":

54 Augmentation

Diminished

Any minor chord can be made into a **diminished** chord by lowering the fifth by a half step. The suffix for a diminished chord is "dim" or "°":

55 Diminished Chords

Suspended

Another common chord variation is the **sus chord** (short for "suspended"). It's called this because you "suspend" the third of the chord with either the **fourth** ("sus") or the **second** ("sus2").

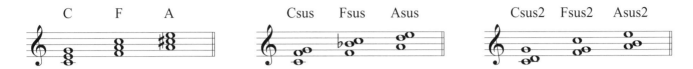

🞤56 Suspension Tension

Sixth

Another common chord type is the **sixth**, aptly named since you play a major or minor chord and simply add the sixth (one whole step higher than the fifth).

This one's not so tense—it's just cool and relaxed sounding:

🞤57 Sixth Sense

Now let's jam with these new chord types:

◆ 58 Laid-Back

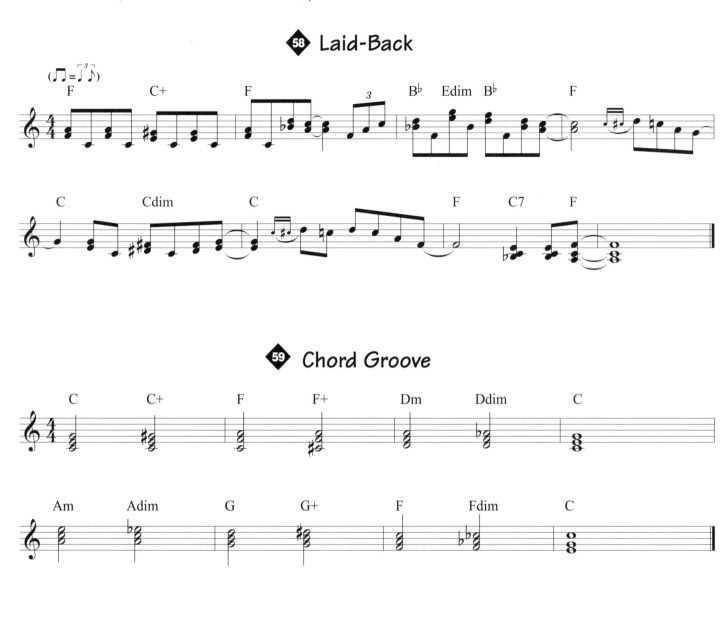

◆ 59 Chord Groove

◆ 60 Metal Vibe

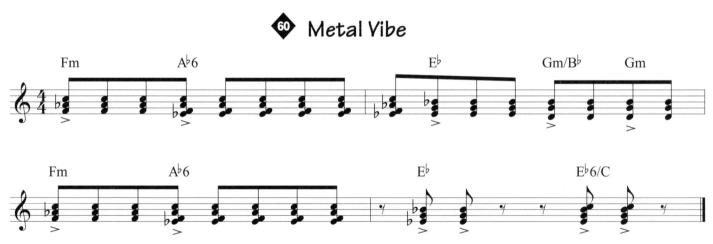

For tons more chords, buy **FastTrack™ Keyboard Chords & Scales**, an excellent supplement book with over 700 chord diagrams, chord theory, and much more.

CALL IN A SUBSTITUTE!

Remember the simple **chord substitution** with minor chords in Lesson 5? Chord substitution means simply replacing the chords of a song with new chords to create a more interesting harmony. Now that you know more chord types, we can try such a technique.

Track 61 is a well-known tune, using a very basic chord progression (I—V7—I):

For a more interesting harmony, find new ways to move from I to V7, using the following approaches:

 Move up **diatonically** (using the scale tones for a new chord root)

      Ex. C—Dm7—Em7—F—G7

 Move up **chromatically** (using the next closest key for a new chord root)

      Ex. C—C#dim—Dm7—G7

 Change to a III7 chord in the second measure and move up in **4th intervals**

      Ex. C—Em7—A7—Dm7—G7—C

Track 62 will show you how to apply each of these approaches to the tune we played above. (Each version will be played twice, followed immediately by the next one.)

Of course, listening is the best way to learn— make up your own substitutions simply by what sounds good to you!

33

LESSON 8

All that jazz...

Now that you're familiar with some new chord types, let's take a look at a musical style that embraces the concept of new chords...

Jazz

An American original—the jazz style features improvisation, complex chord harmony, and a variety of rhythms. Giants like Duke Ellington, Thelonius Monk, and Bill Evans have all been influential in jazz. Many variants have grown from this style, including swing, Dixieland, bebop, Latin-jazz, and fusion.

Generally speaking, anything goes in jazz music. However, there are some common elements—like the **walking bass line.** For track 63, play the chords with your right hand, while your left hand plays single bass notes, represented by the letters above the staff:

63 Walk on Over

For track 64, play the notes below with your left hand. When you've got it, move your left hand down an octave or two and play it again, but this time add the chords with your right hand:

64 Bass Line Jam

IT'S TRICKY: Play just the right-hand chords over and over. Then play just the left-hand bass notes over and over. Then (guess what?) combine the two.

Count on it...

In addition to chord variations, jazz employs lots of cool rhythms. Tap your foot while listening to track 65. (Notice that it uses a swing beat—that is, two eighths are played like a quarter-eighth triplet.)

The first two measures contain the simple eight-note melody that will be repeated seven times, but each time it's repeated there is a new jazzy rhythm.

65 Rhythm Always Changes

Once these jazzy rhythms become familiar to you, apply them to chord progressions, too:

66 Chord Rhythms #1

67 Chord Rhythms #2

LESSON 9

From all corners...

Today's music is influenced by styles from all over the world. Grab your passport and climb aboard...

Reggae

Reggae was born on the small island of Jamaica. This unique music style, played by such legends as Bob Marley and Jimmy Cliff, has been influential on music throughout the world.

Notice the common rhythm used in reggae style—emphasizing beats 2 and 4:

68 Jamaican Me Crazy

Latin

Music from Latin America has been another major influence on dance, pop, and even jazz music. Just like their food, Latin rhythms are fresh, unique, and spicy...

IMPORTANT: Use single notes in the left hand. The letters above the staff represent single notes to be played, not chords.

69 Salsa

Pentatonic

Pentatonic literally means "having five tones." So, you would guess correctly that pentatonic music uses only five tones in its melodies, scales and chord structures. It can be heard in anything from Asian folk tunes to heavy metal riffs.

There are two pentatonic scale patterns you should learn—major and minor.

Major Pentatonic Scale   Minor Pentatonic Scale

Now listen to how these scales work in songs. First, the Asian folk music (major pentatonic)...

72 China Moon

And now the heavy metal riff (minor pentatonic)...

NOTE: A chord that works well with pentatonic is the "5" chord. This is a two-note chord with only the root and fifth. For example, play the notes C and G for a C5 chord.

73 Heavy Keys

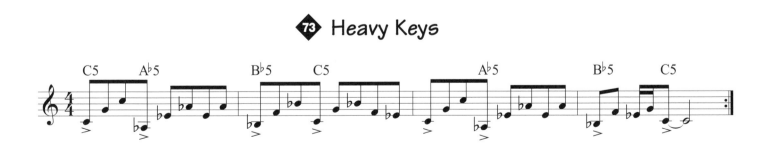

Let's not forget our friends in Nashville—country music dates back from even before rock 'n' roll. Its form is usually simpler and more "laid back," although many of today's country artists like Garth Brooks, Reba McEntire, and Shania Twain incorporate some rock styles in their music.

NOTE: Melodies to many country songs are based on the major pentatonic scale.

74 Notes from Nashville

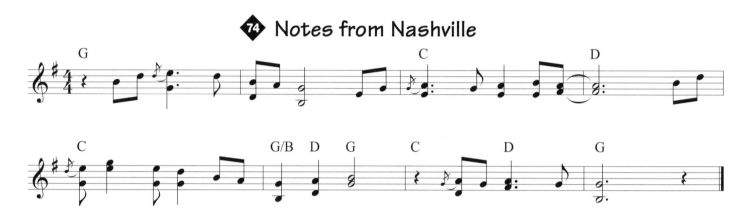

Notice the unique use of intervals and grace notes, which contribute to country music's unmistakable sound:

75 This Must Be Tennessee

A nice accompaniment to a country-style song is to apply a "broken chord" technique with the right hand while the left hand alternates between the chord's root and fifth. For track 76, the letter above the staff indicates **single notes** to play with the left hand (not chords!)...

76 Country Picking

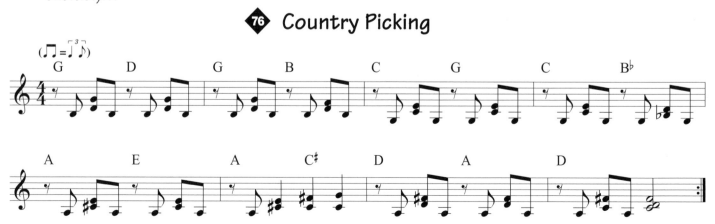

HEY, PONCHO! DON'T FORGET "LEFTY"

Try a different left-hand accompaniment for ballads: play the root, fifth and octave above the root for each chord. Play them one at a time (up and then back down) like the "broken chord" technique in Book 1. Review the diagram below and listen to track 77 for a better understanding of what we mean.

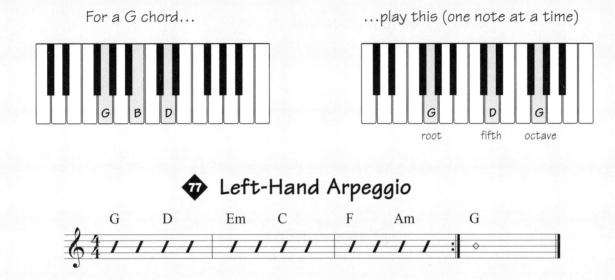

For a G chord...   ...play this (one note at a time)

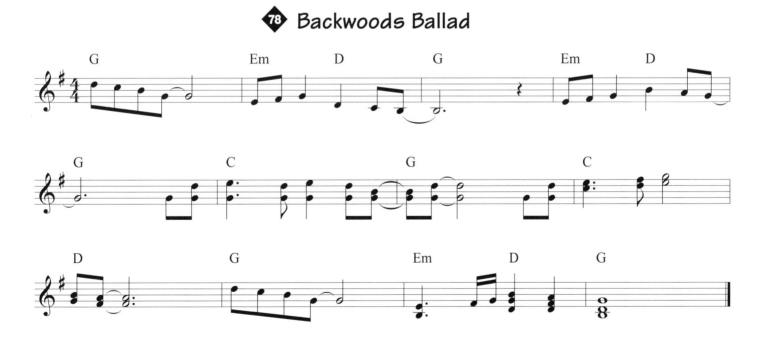

Now apply it to a ballad:

 Time for another break! You owe it to yourself (and to your poor fingers).
Knitting would not be a good activity during this break?!

LESSON 10

Allow us to introduce...

When an "intro" is needed to start a song, who do you think the rest of the band will turn to? That's right—you! Well, throw some of these at them...

🔷79 3/4 Ballad Intro

Try that one again, but slow down the tempo of the last measure.

🔷80 Rock Intro

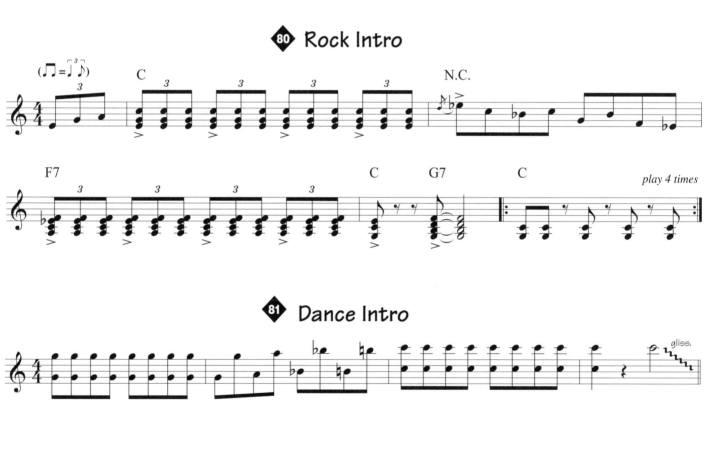

🔷81 Dance Intro

🔷82 Honky-Tonk Intro

Notice the progress...

Create an intro with a simple chord progression that will lead you to the first chord of the song (usually the I chord). Some that work well are:

III—VI—II—V—(I)

I—V—VI—V—V7—(I)

I—III—IV—V7—(I)

HOW TO DO IT: Like the primary chords in Lesson 2, use a key's scale tones to find these numbered chords. (Remember that II, III, and VI are minor and VII is diminished.)

Here are examples of chord progression intros...

 **Chord Intro #1**

 **Chord Intro #2**

Don't forget the broken chord option:

Arpeggio Intro

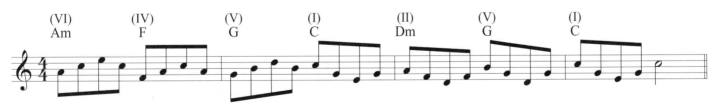

Keep these ideas handy...just in case you're ever asked:
"Hey, Keys! Start us off in G, please!"

Exit stage left...

So, you started the song...now how do you end it? Try some of these fancy outros:

86 Bluesy Outro

87 Ballad Ending

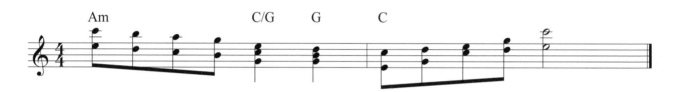

88 Slow and Easy

...and we couldn't resist the ever-popular...

89 Shave and a Haircut

LESSON 11

Strike up the band...

As in the first book, this last section isn't a lesson...it's your jam session!

All the **FastTrack**™ books (Guitar, Keyboard, Bass and Drums) have the same last section. This way, you can either play by yourself along with the audio or form a band with your friends.

So, whether the band's on the audio tracks or in your garage, let the show begin...

E **Drum Break**

F **Outro Chorus**

92 **93** Dim the Lights
full band   minus keys

A **Intro**
Slow Rock ♩. = 58

B **Verse/Chorus**

C **Guitar Solo**

We would be sad that this was the end of our relationship,
but we'll see you again in **FastTrack**™ **Keyboard Songbook 2.**

A FAREWELL GIFT

(...it's the least we could do!)

We expect you to use the entire book as a reference, but this has now become a tradition—a "cheat sheet" with all the chords you learned. Don't forget to practice often!

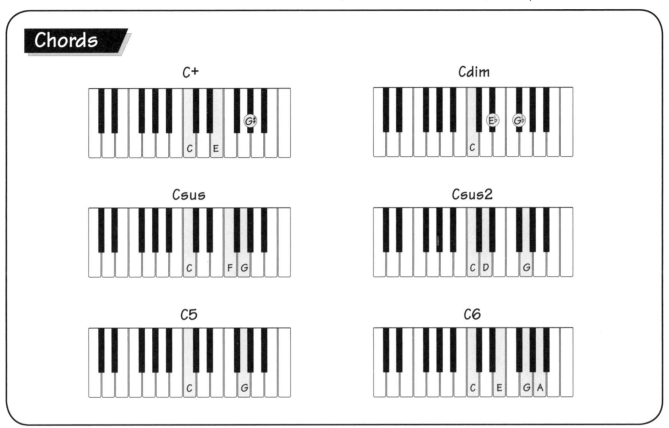

Chords

C+ | Cdim | Csus | Csus2 | C5 | C6

What's next?

You've started to master the keyboard in just a short time, but where do you go now?

 1 **Practice, practice, practice.** Continue to learn by practicing each day.

 2 **Buy FastTrack™ Keyboard Songbooks 1** and **2**, featuring rock score format of hits from Eric Clapton, Elton John, The Beatles, Jerry Lee Lewis, and many more.

 3 **Buy FastTrack™ Keyboard Chords & Scales**, an excellent reference book with over 700 chords and inversions, scale and mode patterns, and popular chord progressions.

 4 **Enjoy what you do.** If you don't enjoy what you're doing, there's no sense in doing it.

Bye for now...

SONG INDEX

(...gotta have one!)